# *Sunset*

# Family Rooms
# & Activity Areas

By the Editors of Sunset Books and Sunset Magazine

*Family room offers cozy quarters by the fire and a quiet spot for watching television, reading, or just relaxing.*
Architect: John Duvivier. Interior design: Sharon Kasser, Distinctive Interiors.

**Lane Publishing Co. ▪ Menlo Park, California**

Book Editor
**Ginger Smith Bate**

Contributing Editors
**Rod Smith**
**Fran Feldman**

Coordinating Editor
**Linda J. Selden**

Design
**Joe di Chiarro**

Illustrations
**Mark Pechenik**

Photo Stylist
**JoAnn Masaoka**

**Photographers: Keeping Traditions,** 94; **Stephen Marley,** 8, 9, 24, 25, 36, 37, 38, 39, 40, 41, 80, 81, 83, 95; **Jack McDowell,** 82; **Tom Wyatt,** 1, 3, 5, 6, 7, 10, 11, 12, 13, 14, 15, 16, 17, 18, 19, 26, 27, 28, 29, 30, 31, 32, 33, 34, 35, 43, 44, 45, 46, 47, 48, 49, 52, 53, 54, 55, 56, 57, 60, 61, 62, 63, 65, 66, 67, 68, 69, 70, 71, 74, 75, 76, 77, 78, 79, 86, 87, 88, 89, 92, 93.

**Cover:** Comfortable and casual, spacious family kitchen combines kitchen, eating area, conversation corner, and study center in one cheerful space. Architect: Donald King Loomis. Interior design: Ruth Livingston. Photographed by Tom Wyatt. Photo styling by JoAnn Masaoka.

Sunset Books
    Editor: David E. Clark
    Managing Editor: Elizabeth L. Hogan

First printing May 1988

## Gathering places & private spaces

Every home has at least one room where the family tends to gather. Sometimes, it's a warm and inviting family kitchen; other times it may be a comfortable family room. Or it may even be a state-of-the-art media center.

As leisure-time activities become more specialized, the rooms that accommodate them often require reorganization, redesign, or even remodeling. Whether you're looking for a home for an extensive collection of books, you need a light, airy space for some gleaming new fitness equipment, or you're replacing an old television with a wide-screen model, you'll find a wealth of designs and ideas in this book which you can adapt to your own situation.

We begin with large, traditional family spaces that serve multiple purposes—family rooms, great rooms, and family kitchens. In the second chapter, we present ideas for more private retreats for quiet pursuits—dens, offices, and libraries. Finally, we feature activity areas for television viewing, exercise, entertaining, and recreation.

As you look at the rooms other families have created, consider the possibilities for your own home. To help you plan, we've included a brief section on remodeling and room conversions; for more specific information, consult the *Sunset* book *Home Remodeling Illustrated.*

*Easy access to patio and backyard makes this sunny*
*family room a popular gathering place for*
*family and friends alike.*
Architect: Architectural Resources Group.
Interior design: Kay Dunne Interiors.

# Contents

## Special Features

# Family Rooms, Great Rooms & Family Kitchens

**F**amily rooms, great rooms, and family kitchens are all variations on the same theme: multifunctional rooms designed for group activity. Whether it's cooking and eating, socializing with family or friends, or just passing a rainy day in quiet diversions, these rooms shine when the gang's all here.

Though their functions may be similar, each room has its own distinct personality. Generally, a family room occupies a separate space in the house; though it may be off the kitchen, no cooking takes place there. A great room, on the other hand, combines the functions of a family room, kitchen, and sometimes even a dining room and living room in one large space; often, there's not even any delineation to mark where one "room" ends and the next one begins.

A more modest version of a great room, a family kitchen provides space for both cooking and socializing, though often the only formal socializing space is the kitchen table and chairs.

***A traditional family room.*** Any room can be a family room, and every house has at least one room where family members tend to gather. Often, a family room is near the kitchen; sometimes, it opens to a patio or to the backyard. A family room can be a comfortable perch in the attic or even a snug refuge in the basement.

Light plays an important role in making the room comfortable and attractive. Sunlight can be welcomed by means of new windows or skylights. When you're considering artificial lighting, note how people use the room; by lighting separate areas discreetly, a family room can be divided into several different spaces without your having to remodel.

Seating needs to be welcoming and convenient, whether the room is used for reading, watching television, playing games, listening to music, or all of the above. And don't neglect storage space—bookshelves, cabinets, drawers, perhaps even a closet—to corral the clutter that accumulates in any frequently used room.

*Overstuffed sofa and chairs upholstered in bold stripes spell comfort in this well-appointed family room. Raised granite hearth reflects glow of fire. Dark wood wall unit accommodates wide-screen television, treasured musical instruments, and family mementos; cabinet doors above television open to reveal stereo equipment.*
Architect: Kwan-Henmi Associates. Interior design: Kelly Associates.

**Creating a great room.** Rapidly gaining in popularity, great rooms are family rooms in the grand sense. The idea dates back centuries to the days when a family lived, slept, cooked, ate, and entertained in one large space, often sharing that space with their livestock. Though sleeping now takes place in a separate area, today's great room is very much in keeping with that tradition.

Remodeling to create a great room may mean opening up the wall between the kitchen and family room or taking down all the walls that separate the kitchen from the family room, living room, and dining room. Either the room can be left as one large space or separate areas can be delineated, perhaps by means of a sunken conversation area, a dining mezzanine, a dropped ceiling, or an entertainment center tucked into an alcove.

As in a separate family room, comfortable seating, good lighting, and adequate storage space lend versatility to the room, whether it's being used for a family evening at home or to entertain guests before dinner.

*At any time of day, light is dramatic in this great room, thanks to a skylight and walls of windows. Both kitchen and dining area open onto a tree-shaded patio. Counter with stools and table and chairs provide two eating areas. Sofa is perfect for reading or quiet conversations.*
*Architect: Robert Peterson, Architects, Inc.*

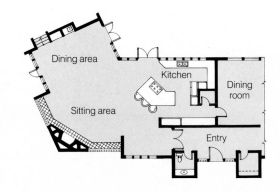

**Gathering in a family kitchen.** There's no place more popular among family members than the kitchen, so it often makes sense to extend or enlarge the kitchen into another kind of family space.

A family kitchen usually includes an informal eating area—a counter with stools, a kitchen table, or perhaps both. A contiguous seating area, if there's room, makes the kitchen a convenient place to socialize out of the cook's way and may even provide an entertainment area suitable for small groups. Adding a desk to a family kitchen allows the cook to keep track of the activities of family members as well as of their nutrition.

A good choice for storage in a family kitchen is a wall-mounted unit that takes up no floor space, yet provides shelves and cabinets for a television, books, stereo system, tapes, and games. Task lighting, such as a fixture over the kitchen table or a lamp next to a reading chair, can both help keep the spaces separate and offer the lighting necessary for the different activities taking place there.

*Cheery family kitchen occupies a single large space, yet keeps multiple functions carefully separated. Polished oak flooring, light wood, and compatible colors unify design.*
Interior design: Elizabeth Hill, Selby House.

# Balancing Act

*This high-ceilinged breakfast area and sunken hearthside family room share common space, yet maintain different identities.*

**Handsome display shelving divides breakfast area from sunken seating area. Window seat at right of fireplace covers a storage bin for firewood.**

**Gable window and skylight flood breakfast area with light that spills into sunken seating area. Pass-through at left is service shortcut to kitchen.**
*Architect: Hiro Morimoto.*

# Rooms with Horizons

*Glass walls and roofs take family rooms into the great outdoors without sacrificing comfort.*

*Sunny alcove off kitchen integrates built-in seating, storage, fireplace, and television, making the most of limited space.*
Architect: Paul R. Rotter.

*White-framed French doors (top) open to gardenlike atrium. Lofty house plants thrive in bright, glassed-in space, link inside with out-of-doors (at right). Earthen tile floor and neutral color scheme enhance outdoor feeling.*
Architect: Paul R. Rotter.
Interior design: Helen Reed Craddick.

# Open to View

When no interior design can compete with the splendor of what's outside, the solution is an elegant enclosure that captures the view through walls of windows.

One side of L-shaped great room is a formal sitting room with fireplace. Concealed lights illuminate objects on shelves flanking chimney. Ceiling spots take over lighting duties when the sun sets.

*Light wood floor and off-white walls
and ceiling provide a neutral palette
for shifting light and colors outside.
Combined work/storage peninsula
and breakfast bar (at left) expands
kitchen work space and divides it
from dining area; strong, clean lines
of open-beamed ceiling
smooth transition.*
Architect: William B. Remick. Interior
design: Jane Howerton Interiors.

# Near, Yet Far Away

*Three distinct spaces marked off with partial walls merge into one large great room, thanks to earthy tile floor, subdued colors, and unified design scheme.*

**Hand-painted urn and marble sculpture work with columns to at once define and unify living and dining areas.**

*Light floods great room through tall
windows in daytime; at night, table
lamp, track lighting, and fixture over
dining room table provide diverse
illumination.*
Design: Robert A. Staehle.

Great Rooms **15**

# Whites Make Light

*Shining white surfaces, juxtaposed with off-white, bleached wood, amplify light from several sources to make this great room glow.*

*Fireside seating area flows comfortably from kitchen, echoes colors and materials. Cabinets flanking fireplace store books, a stereo system, and video equipment.*

*Windowless kitchen benefits from high ceiling, skylights, strategically placed track lighting, and bright surfaces. Island, focal point of kitchen, unifies space, also acts as a boundary line.*
Interior design: Jean Gatch Ashby.

# View from the Bridge

*Half-wall of raised platform in this spacious great room hides kitchen, yet allows everyone to enjoy the magnificent view.*

*From sunken family room, kitchen is barely obvious. Built-in cabinetry wraps around platform wall, providing ample shelf space.*

*White, eye-level counter (above) allows cook to look out but hides food preparation from view. Sleek stainless-steel countertops, efficient work spaces, and louvered cabinet doors (at right) nearly disguise true purpose of room. When stools are added, island becomes a casual eating area.*

Architect: Peter C. Rodi, Designbank.

Family room

Dining room

Kitchen

Nook

# Redefining Space with a Remodel or Room Conversion

**A**s your family grows and changes through the years, your house needs to change, too. Most often the need for more space is paramount, but new interests or occupations, such as a business run out of your home, may require that you redefine the space you already have. Most houses are veritable gold mines of underutilized space that can be drafted into service or, as in the case of an attic, garage, or basement, changed from one use to another.

Reassigning interior space often involves changes that affect the basic structure of the house, such as removing walls or raising ceilings. Converting an existing space to a different use has fewer structural ramifications but still may require extensive work.

***Basic house structure.*** If you're considering structural changes, it's essential to have a basic understanding of the structural shell of your house. Starting at the base of the drawing shown below (at left), you'll notice the following framing members: a wooden sill resting on a foundation wall; a series of horizontal, evenly spaced floor joists; and a subfloor (usually plywood sheets) laid atop the joists. This platform supports the first-floor walls, which are formed by vertical, evenly spaced studs that run between a horizontal sole plate and parallel top

## Basic House Anatomy

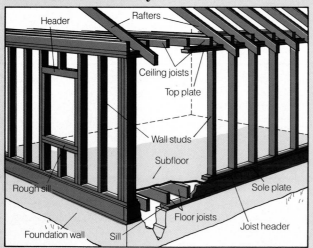

*It's important to have a solid working knowledge of structural anatomy before launching a remodeling project. This drawing shows the basic elements of wood frame construction.*

## Bearing & Nonbearing Walls

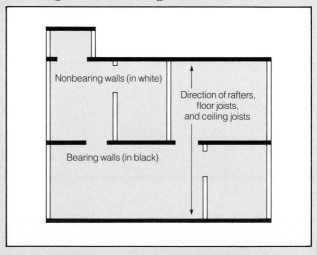

*Bearing walls, which help support the weight of the structure, are harder to move than nonbearing walls. Note that both types may conceal ducts, wires, and pipes that will need to be rerouted.*

plate. The primary wall coverings are fastened directly to the studs.

If there's a second story, a layer of ceiling joists rests on the walls; these joists support both the floor above and the ceiling below.

A one-story house will have either an open-beamed ceiling—flat or pitched—or a finished ceiling. In simple terms, a finished ceiling covers the roof rafters and sheathing which, if exposed, would constitute an open-beamed ceiling. With a flat roof, the finished ceiling is attached directly to the rafters. The ceiling below a pitched roof is attached to joists.

The walls of your house are either bearing or nonbearing (see drawing on facing page, at right). The former help support the weight of the house; the latter do not. All exterior walls running perpendicular to floor and ceiling joists are bearing, and normally at least one interior wall, situated over a girder or interior foundation wall, will also be bearing. The function of a particular wall can be determined by looking at a blueprint; if none is available, consult a building contractor or structural engineer.

If you decide to move or alter a bearing wall, you'll have to provide permanent support around the opening. And any wall, whether bearing or nonbearing, probably hides a network of heating ducts, electrical wires, and plumbing pipes, all of which will have to be rerouted.

Of course, a room conversion also presents challenges, especially if you need to bring electricity, heat, or plumbing into an area where it does not already exist. However, converting an attic into a home office can not only free space below but also provide a quiet retreat for serious work. Descending into the basement makes sense for a fitness room, well lit, heated, and furnished with mats, fixed exercise equipment, and perhaps a shower or spa. The garage, usually located off the kitchen, offers potential as a family room or, with the wall opened up, a great room.

***Moving up into the attic.*** In an unfinished attic, you'll be dealing with wide fluctuations of temperature, limited access, poor light, and either a flimsy subfloor or none at all. Also, the space likely has an awkward shape, with steeply slanting walls rendering a large percentage of the floor space practically useless. Moreover, ducts, vents, and wires are probably exposed, and there may be a chimney to work around.

You'll need to insulate and finish the walls, lay a sturdy subfloor, and install windows and/or skylights for light and ventilation. Fans will help with additional ventilation, if necessary. Heat can be pro-

vided by extending the home's existing system or by installing a wall heater.

Will access need to be improved? If all you have is a hatch in the ceiling, you'll need to think about stairs. Though spiral staircases are the most compact in terms of space, they're awkward to use and are sometimes banned by local building codes. The more maneuverable straight staircase takes up a fair amount of space and may entail further structural changes (such as opening up a large stairwell), so you'll need to plan its location carefully.

Explore lighting possibilities with a free imagination, because light plays a major role in a room's personality. If left exposed, an attic's roof ridge and rafters are ready-made for strip lighting, tracks, or hanging grids. A combination of light sources works effectively: concealed strips for general illumination and focused beams to highlight a desk, an easel, or a sitting area. Note that you may have to add an additional 15- or 20-amp circuit if your existing system isn't sufficient to handle the extra demand.

(Continued on next page)

## Activating an Attic

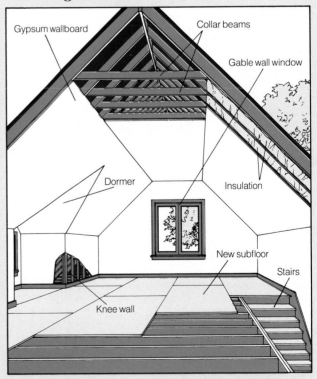

*Converting an attic to livable space may be relatively simple. By introducing insulation, wall coverings, a solid floor, and windows, a rough and irregular space can be transformed into a comfortable room.*

*...continued from page 21*

**Basement spaces.** The basement presents some of the attic's problems (poor light, for example), along with some unique to underground spaces, especially excessive moisture from a seeping foundation or sweating pipes. Headroom may also be a problem.

Poor light can be corrected fairly easily with the addition of light fixtures, but importing natural light into a basement that's below grade level may be difficult. One possibility is a light well, created by excavating a pit next to the foundation and opening the wall for a window. This is not a project to be undertaken lightly (consult a structural engineer to see if it's feasible); moreover, it will probably be quite expensive. Still, a picture window below ground level, perhaps looking onto a lush garden, can transform a basement fitness room or office into a cozy retreat.

To gain headroom, you may be able to lower a section of the floor, but consider that a last resort. Since equipment access is limited, excavation and debris removal must be done by hand—and a 3-inch-thick concrete slab doesn't give itself up easily.

You can handle minor moisture problems from the inside by applying masonry sealer to halt seepage through walls and floor. Sweating pipes can be wrapped in special jackets and vapor barriers. But if you can actually *see* water leaking through your basement wall, you'll probably have to stem the flow of water at its source outside the house.

If your basement isn't heated already, you may be able to run new ducts to the basement space. To finish up, you'll need to insulate the walls and apply the appropriate floor and wall coverings.

Overhead framing, pipes, and ductwork can often be hidden by dropping the ceiling, if there's sufficient headroom, or by installing acoustic tiles or wallboard. Or you can simply leave the joists exposed.

**Expanding into the garage.** The garage presents fewer obstacles to conversion and remodeling than the attic or basement. It's accessible, is located at ground level, and offers a large, unobstructed space. It probably has electricity already, with water and heat not far off. But be sure to check your local

## Upgrading a Basement

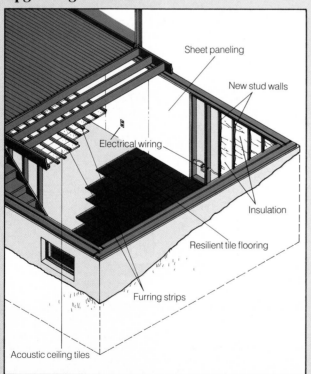

Sheet paneling

New stud walls

Electrical wiring

Insulation

Resilient tile flooring

Furring strips

Acoustic ceiling tiles

*With just minimal improvement, a basement makes an ideal retreat. A new ceiling, floor, and wall covering can turn space into a study, home office, or family room. Be sure to guard against seepage.*

## Garage Conversion

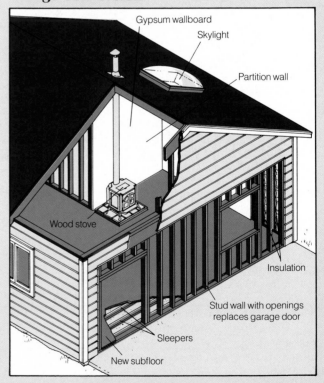

Gypsum wallboard

Skylight

Partition wall

Wood stove

Insulation

Stud wall with openings replaces garage door

Sleepers

New subfloor

*Warmth and light—from a wood-burning stove and a skylight—enhance a garage conversion. With basic elements in place, creativity can take over to make the new space inviting.*

building code before banishing the car elsewhere; in many areas, covered spaces must be provided for cars.

A major concern in a garage conversion is what to do with the garage door. If you decide to remove it, you'll need to frame in the wall, taking the opportunity to introduce windows or perhaps sliding glass doors. Or, you can leave the door in place, camouflaging it by refinishing the exterior and interior walls entirely or by covering the door itself with siding and wall material that matches what's already there.

Before applying any flooring to the slab, make sure it's level and completely dry; if not, apply a vapor barrier and build a subfloor. The walls can be finished as desired.

***Converting a porch or patio.*** Turning a framed porch into an extra room may be as simple as adding windows and, perhaps, lighting and heat. Turning a paved patio into living space, on the other hand, may be as much work as adding an entirely new room.

Even if the porch has an adequate foundation, you still may have to deal with building up the floor, installing insulation, supplying ventilation, and bringing in wiring, heating ducts, and possibly plumbing. And you'll want to finish the exterior to match the house.

Patio conversion is much more difficult than porch conversion. If the foundation does not meet building codes, you'll virtually be starting from scratch and adding a new room.

## Steps in Remodeling

Before you begin your project, it's important to have a clear idea of the sequence of steps necessary to complete the job. The larger the project, the greater the need for careful planning. Before work begins, double-check the priorities listed below:

- Establish the sequence of jobs to be performed in the remodel and estimate the time required to complete each one.

- If you're getting professional assistance for any part of the work, make sure you have firm contracts and schedules with contractors, subcontractors, or other hired workers.

- Obtain all required building permits. (To find out what building codes may affect your remodeling project and whether or not a building permit is required, check with your city or county building department.)

- Arrange for delivery of materials; be sure you have all the necessary tools on hand.

- If electricity, gas, or water must be shut off by the utility company, arrange for it before work is scheduled to begin.

- Find out where you can dispose of refuse and secure any necessary dumping permits. Or rent your own dumpster.

- Be sure there's a storage area available for temporarily relocating furniture, fixtures, appliances, and any other possessions that will be in the way of the remodel.

- Measure fixtures and appliances for clearance through doorways and up and down staircases.

You can use the lists below to plan the basic sequence of tasks involved in taking apart the area being remodeled and in putting it back together again. Depending on the scale of your job and the specific materials you select, you may need to alter the suggested order or perhaps even skip some steps.

Your goal is to maintain an operating household during as much of the time as possible. With careful scheduling and planning, the remodeling time can be relatively comfortable for the entire family.

### Removal sequence

1. Accessories, decorative elements
2. Furniture
3. Contents of cabinets, closets, shelves
4. Fixtures, appliances
5. Countertops, backsplashes
6. Cabinets, shelves
7. Flooring materials
8. Light fixtures
9. Wall coverings
10. Wiring, plumbing, heating
11. Framing

### Installation sequence

1. Structural changes: walls, doors, windows, skylights
2. Rough utility changes: wiring, plumbing, heating
3. Wall and ceiling coverings
4. Light fixtures
5. Cabinets, shelves
6. Countertops, backsplashes
7. Flooring materials
8. Fixtures, appliances
9. Furniture
10. Accessories, decorative elements

# Back to Nature

*Expansive windows take cooking, dining, and socializing to new heights in this great room with a view.*

*Wide, fixed-glass windows enclose former deck, bringing nature indoors and putting diners at treetop level. Slight step-down and raised ceiling in garden room enlarge space. Uniform surfaces and colors throughout tie elements together.*

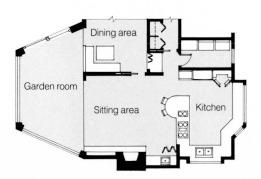

**Plants in front of vista windows (above) usher lush garden into great room, seemingly without interruption. Location of kitchen at closed end of great room (at left) keeps it separate from traffic while allowing everyone to get involved.**
*Architect: Donald King Loomis.*
*Interior design: Ruth Livingston.*

# A Touch of Brass

*By sunlight or firelight, restrained use of shiny brass in this multipurpose great room brings out highlights in natural wood finishes.*

**Traffic through great room circulates outside cooking area, past bar and fireplace to dining bay.**

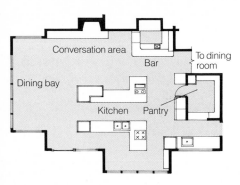

Conversation area

Bar

To dining room

Dining bay

Kitchen    Pantry

*Antique dining table (at left) is embraced by garden outside bay. After dark, brass nautical lanterns fill alcove with intimate reflected light, illuminate path outside. In kitchen area (below), gleaming brass hood trimmed with copper casts a warm glow.*
*Architect: J. Allen Sayles.*

# Arches & Alcoves

*Colorful tile and repeated arch motif evoke a Mediterranean feeling in this spacious great room.*

*A variety of materials—brick, polished woods, painted tile, and gleaming copper—blend warmly in eat-in kitchen. Cooktop nestles in its own lighted alcove at rear. Desk and phone fit into another arched recess at right.*

*Formal seating area on lower level is perfectly positioned for viewing wide-screen television. When not in use, it hides behind handsome cabinetry that matches kitchen's.*
Architect: Peter C. Rodi, Designbank.

# A Study in Black & White

*Ultramodern step-down family kitchen in crisp black and white gains space from tall windows and high, sculptured ceiling.*

*Gleaming polished granite countertops reflect abundant natural light in both kitchen and breakfast nook. Short stairway leads out to patio and view.*

*Unexpected angles, dramatic use of color, and rich slate tile floor lend excitement to businesslike kitchen.*
*Architect: Rob Wellington Quigley.*

# Harvest Home

*Expanses of natural wood, antique wooden furniture, and soft accent colors characterize this country-style family kitchen.*

*Working columns subtly define space, add intimacy to traditional dining area and modern kitchen just steps away.*

*Cozy window seat with storage beneath adds a note of informality to spacious, open-ceilinged dining area.*
Architect: William B. Remick.

# An Affair of the Hearth

*Simple fireplace unifies eating and food preparation areas in spacious, stylishly traditional family kitchen.*

*Family kitchen hums with activity at mealtime. Several people can cook together comfortably, while onlookers taste-test and kibitz.*

**Hard-working peninsula divider is centerpiece of kitchen. Desk and eating counter are on social side, sink and work space on business side. Tile in kitchen matches hearth.**
*Architect: William B. Remick.*

# Elements of Style

*Yankee tradition meets modern design in this charming, highly efficient family kitchen.*

*Rain or shine, this genteel family kitchen is a natural gathering place. Parlor tricks that make the most out of limited space include companion seating in window bay and pine floor polished to softly reflect both sun and firelight.*

*Brick wall in efficient, modern kitchen echoes traditional feeling of eating area. Two-way pine counter separates spaces, makes serving easy.*
Architect: Ken Whitehead.

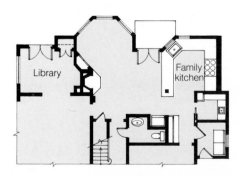

# Best Seats in the House

*Elevated breakfast area puts family and friends at ringside, but conveniently out of the cook's way.*

*Daylight floods this comfortable family kitchen through a bay window to left of eating/cooking peninsula (see photo at right). White board ceiling, clear finishes, and gleaming dark granite countertops reflect light to show off dishes and glassware in open shelving.*

*Mezzanine is near action, yet far enough away to prevent interference.*
*Working kitchen is convenient to both mezzanine and formal dining room,*
*through door at left.*
Architect: William B. Remick.

# A Shining Example

*Lots of light, plenty of white, and pale complementary shades lend serenity to this pristine family kitchen.*

*Kitchen traffic circulates around multipurpose island, which provides areas for cooking and eating along with easy-access storage. Skylights and track lighting along angled beams supplement sidelighting from window over sink.*

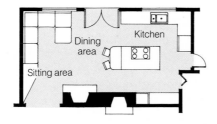

*Family lounge puts media center next to cooking area, making kitchen the center of activity. Television, which slides out and swivels a full 90°, brings "great chefs" into family kitchen. Built-in wall and seating unit provides generous storage space at floor level.*
Interior design: Ruth Livingston.

Dining area

Kitchen

Sitting area

# Dens, Offices & Libraries

Families differ, and the way they use their homes differs, too. Sometimes, it's desirable to dedicate a space to such a specific use as a den, home office, or library. Each of these adds versatility to a home at the same time that it provides a comfortable retreat that meets a particular need.

***Dens—private retreats.*** A den is everything the name implies: a private, comfortable place for relaxation removed from the frantic pace of life outside. The den is a place to read, watch television, listen to music, sort through the mail, or just talk.

Because the den often has the air of an inner sanctum, a kind of private club for family members only, it's best located in a quiet part of the house. Let other rooms handle crowds—the den is more exclusive, the perfect place for a favorite chair, a good reading lamp, some books, and perhaps even a small desk. A fireplace or wood-burning stove can add ambience.

You can bring in natural light through a bay window and build in a comfortable alcove bench for seating beneath. Convert the space under the bench into a roomy storage compartment or use more conventional shelves and cabinets. And by all means include bookshelves in the plan. The den is the logical place to keep books, from mysteries and adventure stories to dog-eared gardening references of the type that see most of their action on cozy evenings in the dead of winter.

***An office at home.*** As modern life gets ever more complicated, many families find the need for an office in the home, perhaps even one that can be shared by two people.

Such a room can play a surprisingly central role in family life. It's an obvious place to set up a computer workstation that can be used by all members of the family; it's also a good place for the home's telephone answering machine and a bulletin board for

*Paneled treetop retreat handles weighty matters with aplomb. Carved wood conference table invites serious business discussions; red leather chairs provide for comfortable reading of library selections. Small personal computer settles easily into its traditional surroundings.*

Architect: Kwan-Henmi Associates. Interior design: Kelly Associates.

messages. You might want to run a pair of stereo speakers from a system elsewhere in the home to enliven long evenings spent poring over bank statements.

Good light is crucial in a home office, particularly if it's headquarters for a business or a serious student. Aim for diffuse, soft illumination that avoids high contrast between your work area and its surroundings, particularly if you're working at a dark computer screen. Task lighting, artificial light focused directly on a certain area, should be sufficiently strong to prevent eyestrain, yet carefully controlled to avoid glare.

Built-ins are particularly well suited to home offices. Not only do they allow you to design spaces that are tailored to your specific needs, but they also lend a more formal, businesslike appearance to the room. Be sure to include drawers for files, shelves for books and manuals, and storage for office supplies. If there's room, you may want to add some comfortable chairs or even a large conference table.

**Hall office takes advantage of sunlight from patio and poolside windows and doors. Built-in shelves are both functional and decorative; cabinets provide additional storage space. When opened, French doors ensure ventilation, create a sense of working outdoors.**
*Architect: Richard Brayton, Charles Pfister Associates.*

*Sunlight pouring through louvered doors and windows is decorative accent in this congenial den. Ceiling fan, terra-cotta tiles, and pueblo-style fireplace add to high-desert simplicity.*
Architect: Robert A. Staehle.

**Libraries.** If you have books languishing in boxes in a basement, attic, or closet, you may want to convert part of the house from general use to a library. It doesn't have to take up an entire room; any location where there are more than a few books on display, and accessible, qualifies as a library.

Ideally, the library will be a resource for the whole family, with books organized in a meaningful way. A library can be as large as an entire room lined with shelves and equipped with stools for getting to the top titles, or as compact and specialized as a collection of cook books in the family kitchen.

A bookcase with adjustable shelves that can accommodate everything from small paperbacks to large picture books is a good choice for a library. Be sure also that light levels both at night and during the day are adequate for reading. Downlights that illuminate the bookshelves will make choosing volumes easier and more comfortable. For more information on designing bookshelves, see page 58.

# The Comforts of Home

*Large or small, these quiet retreats,
decorated in subdued colors, are special
places for whiling away time.*

*Whether it's for study, quiet
conversation, eating, or just
contemplation, this peaceful guest-
house room rises to the occasion.*
Design: Robert A. Staehle.

*Snug den, utilizing space effectively, offers comfortable seating, open and closed storage, fireplace, and media center. Kitchen pass-through at right doubles as an informal eating bar.*
Design: Teri's Interior Design Consultants.

Dens **47**

# Fine & Private Places

Save dramatic effects for other rooms in the house—these dens make the most of family quiet time by being cozy, versatile, and easy on the eyes.

*White-washed brick, earth-toned hearth tile, and pale woven carpeting set the inviting mood in this high-ceilinged den. It's equally pleasant by fireside in cold months and with patio doors wide open in summer.*
Architect: Robert Peterson.

*Elegant dark wood paneling sets off framed prints in this cozy, yesteryear retreat off living room. Sliding small-paned doors shut out distractions while maintaining visual contact with rest of house.*

# Fireplaces & Wood Stoves

**H**earth and home—the two have been partners since the first wily little flame was contained by a human being ages ago. Today it would be possible for someone to live an entire lifetime without seeing an actual flame, and yet most of us go out of our way to make fire a part of our lives.

At home, this can be done with either a fireplace or a wood-burning stove. Basically a firebox with exposed flames, a fireplace is designed to bring warmth and cheer into a room. It can be a conventional structural installation, a heat-circulating type (designed to radiate heat back into the room), or a freestanding unit. Wood-burning stoves, on the other hand, are always freestanding; their flames are contained in a carefully vented metal firebox designed to generate—and radiate—intense heat by means of super-efficient combustion.

Both a fireplace and a wood stove must have a chimney or flue to keep oxygen moving and to draw off smoke and fumes. Because the stove's flue is always exposed (rather than encased in brick or concrete, as with a fireplace), its installation is a matter of particular concern. Many states and communities regulate the use, design, and installation of wood stoves. Be sure to consult the proper authorities early in the planning process.

***Design choices.*** Now that fire is no longer essential, in most cases, for warmth and cooking, we're free to indulge our fantasies when planning for a fireplace or wood stove. Like a jewel, the contained fire can be displayed in practically any setting the imagination can contrive. Freestanding fireplaces come in a range of heating capacities and geometric shapes. Some built-ins are set flush with walls; others project partway or completely into a room (see at right).

A skillful mason, given the wide variety of granites, marbles, and fieldstones available today, can create a traditional fireplace of Killarney or Flor-ence in a contemporary American home. Metal, wood, and brick also lend themselves to a wide range of styles.

If heat is the primary reason for bringing fire into the home, consider the more efficient wood-burning stoves. They come in a practically infinite array of styles, configurations, and capacities, from

## Locating a Fireplace

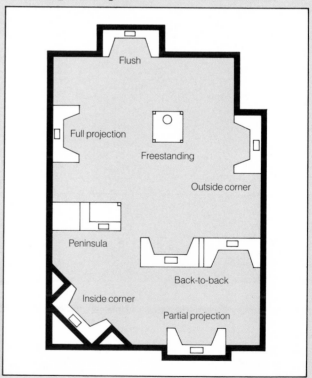

Flush

Full projection

Freestanding

Outside corner

Peninsula

Back-to-back

Inside corner

Partial projection

*This room diagram shows an array of possible fireplace locations. Your choice will depend on traffic patterns and available space in room. Also consider chimney location.*

tiny hall warmers to iron monsters capable of heating large barns. Combining old principles with new technology, wood stoves can generate a tremendous amount of heat with surprisingly little fuel—and manage to look great, too, whether the design is contemporary or traditionally ornate.

***Planning considerations.*** There are several things to think about before installing either a fireplace or a wood stove. Size is one of them. A little heat goes a long way in a properly insulated room, and a fire can easily overpower a space it was meant to make inviting. Be sure to allow for adequate ventilation.

You must be very exacting when locating a wood stove, especially in regard to the distance between the stove-chimney unit and any combustible materials. The pad on which the stove sits and the walls nearest to it take the brunt of radiant heat. By providing extra heat protection all around the stove, you can move it closer to the walls and floor and still maintain proper clearance. (For standard minimum clearances, see the drawing below. Be sure to check the manufacturer's instructions, as well as your local building code.)

When placing fire in a room, think about the flow of traffic. Where are the doors? Where do people tend to sit, stand, or gather? A fire should be centrally located but still be out of the way.

Child safety is also a concern, particularly with wood-burning stoves. A fireplace can be glassed in and the doors locked, but a stove, which is meant to be exposed and to radiate heat, is a potential safety hazard in a home where toddlers are at large. You can surround the stove with a freestanding safety gate, but be careful not to choose one made from plastic, which may melt, or metal, which will conduct the heat and become just as dangerous as the stove itself.

Finally, remember to make provision for feeding the fire. The wood supply should not be so far away that replenishing the blaze detracts from the enjoyment of it.

## Safety Precautions for Wood Stoves

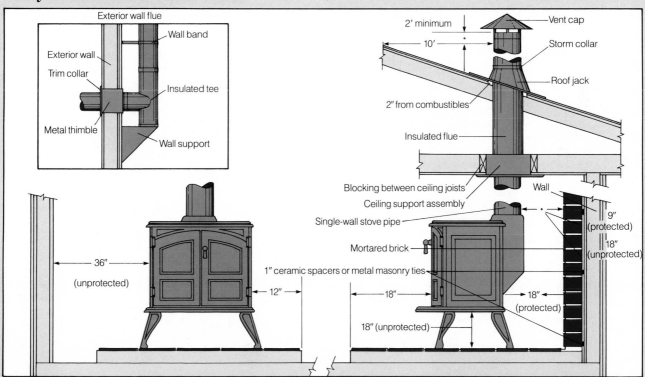

*Wood stoves and their stovepipes require adequate insulation and support for safe operation. Bricks and tiles on pad must be mortared against dropping embers. Minimum clearances shown are those set forth by the National Fire Protection Association; they may differ from those specified by stove manufacturers or local building codes.*

# Home Sweet Office

*Home offices combine comforts and convenience of home with efficiency and organization of business.*

*Skylight sheds benign illumination on polished wood and massed books, inspiring confidence and ease. Magazine rack takes advantage of narrow space beside door. Built-in desk can be used easily from either side.*
*Architect: Raymond M. Rooker. Interior design: Ruth Soforenko Associates.*

*Downstairs reception area welcomes clients with its soft, disarming atmosphere, while loft provides seclusion for hard-working office upstairs. Two levels allow for independent work spaces. Gable window lights desk area.*
Interior design: Rela's Homework.

# Models of Economy

*Less is more in these compact home offices, where economical arrangement and an eye to detail make the most of limited areas.*

*Even the light is subdued in this toned-down home office. Sleek, businesslike presence of desk and podium is softened by overstuffed sofa.*
Interior design: Ruth Livingston.

*Mirror-image desk arrangement (above) turns one end of master bedroom into a roomy office for two. Room divider displays books, stores office supplies on one side, clothes on the other. Gable at far end of office (at right) becomes a sitting/reading nook with addition of pillows and a comfortable futon.* Interior design: Ruth Soforenko Associates.

# Office Hideaways

Built-in cabinetry supports computer work centers in these home offices. Creative use of space is what sets them apart.

*Computer workstation (at right) emerges miraculously from handsome wood cabinets. Disk drive and monitor share space with software manuals. Deep, open-sided drawer holds printer and paper; keyboard slides out on its own shelf. When system is down, it disappears and office reverts to traditional mode (below). Writing desk faces bookshelves in corner enlivened by gleaming glassware over wet bar.*

Furniture design: Interior Design Works, Ltd.

*Plenty of elbow room keeps adjoining workstations (at right) separated in spacious office adjoining master bedroom. Chairs can be moved around to table for head-to-head meetings. Linear arrangement of desks and supporting cabinetry around room (below) maximizes space. Recessed ceiling spots direct light for work and reading.*
Architect: Pierre Prodis.

# Bringing Books to Light

Isn't it odd that bookshelves are often ignored in home design? Books add so much to family life, particularly to eager young minds; yet all too often the family library resides on a few out-of-the-way, dimly lit shelves.

Books are useless if they are not easily accessible. A successful home design brings as many volumes as practical, as discreetly as possible, into the mainstream of daily life. With space at a premium, devoting an entire room to a library may be impractical, but it's easy to integrate books into the household by spreading them throughout the house in a number of small libraries, each holding subject matter appropriate to the activity in that area.

Obviously, cook books have their rightful place in or near the kitchen, where they can be readily consulted. Dickens, Shakespeare, and other classics belong near the fireplace, current best-sellers in the family room, den, or bedroom. How-to guides and technical manuals should be near workbenches and in home offices, and magazines (organized in stacks or binders) need to be stored in the basement or garage.

One common error to avoid is keeping books in the dark. While direct sunlight and too much heat from fireplaces, wood stoves, or radiators can damage books, good light is necessary for browsing through titles, as well as for reading. If possible, locate your bookshelves where they'll benefit from natural light from windows and skylights. Good artificial light sources include track lighting and clip-on fixtures that light shelves from above and from the sides, allowing readers to peruse the books without throwing shadows on the titles.

Locations for bookshelves will no doubt suggest themselves. Look for odd or unused corners or blank sections of walls. Stairwells are an often overlooked source of possibilities, both for shelves that rise alongside the steps (see at right) and for those that are recessed under the stairs. A ledge around a room, just at arm's reach, can hold dozens of books.

*The basics of bookshelf construction.* Building bookshelves is a simple matter of horizontals (the shelves) and verticals (the support system). But before you build, take the following dynamics into account: for light loads, such as small books and art

## Up the Staircase

*Putting a stretch of neglected wall to work, stairside bookshelf accommodates dozens of volumes and takes advantage of overhead lighting already in place.*
Architect: Peter Behn.

## Bookshelf as Room Divider

*Functioning both as a bookshelf and as a room divider, this compartmentalized unit holds books and much more. You can make it from plywood. Store heavy objects near the bottom to guard against tipping.*

objects, you can use 1-by pine or fir supported every 32 inches. For such medium-weight loads as paperbacks, decrease the maximum span to 24 inches and reinforce the boards' edges with 1 by 2 lips. Longer spans and such heavy loads as bound or oversize books and major electronic components require 2-by lumber or two layers of plywood with reinforced edges.

Note that ¾-inch particleboard will sag under its own weight if it spans more than 24 inches; however, most hardwoods and ¾-inch plywood will remain true at 36 inches.

For books of average size, allow at least 9 inches of height and 8 inches of depth; make a section or two 12 inches high for oversize volumes. Record albums require shelves that are 13 inches high. A rule of thumb for shelf capacity is 8 to 10 books per running foot of shelf space.

**Bookshelf design.** Freestanding bookshelves can be as elementary as stacked bricks and boards or as elaborate as a self-contained bookcase with an interior divider and adjustable shelves. Or you can attach shelves directly to the wall with brackets, braces, or tracks that are screwed into wall studs. Choose a style and material that will be compatible with the decor of the room.

Bookshelves are particularly well suited to doing double duty as room dividers, as shown at left. In this unit, the addition of facings on one or both sides creates the look of a solid wall while leaving open niches for decoration. There's still lots of room for books, audio equipment, art objects, and even plants. If you like, you can attach clear acrylic plastic doors to the shelves to keep dust off the books.

A family with an extensive collection of books may want to consider the unconventional arrangement pictured below. Deep steps, many of which run the length of the wall, graduate up to a cozy reading loft just beneath the ceiling. Bookshelves are tucked under the steps, some of which are wide enough for browsing. Just add some soft cushions and provide plenty of good light and your at-home library is complete.

For more detailed information on designing and building bookshelves, consult the *Sunset* book *Bookshelves & Cabinets.*

## Pyramid of Learning

*Each step of this ingenious pyramid is a shelf for books; some are also platforms for reading. Quick vertical rise leads to sunny window ledge at top.*
*Architect: Judith Chafee.*

# A Good Fit

*Gleaming dark wood is not only handsome but also helps to reduce eyestrain when used on desk and countertops. Light in this office/library illuminates without glaring.*

*Elegant built-in units shown below and at right artfully follow curves of walls, fit snugly into alcoves. Custom features include capacious file drawers and large reading podium.*

*Recessed downlights over bookshelves provide soft illumination both for selecting books and for reading. Glazed wall admits copious amounts of natural light by day.*
Architect: Rob Wellington Quigley.

# Making Room for Books

*Plain or fancy, bookshelves take up little space, keep worlds of knowledge on standby for a student, cook, or home-based professional.*

***Impressive collection of books in classic library cases is protected behind glass doors that swing up and slide back to make volumes available.***

*Handsome, wood-paneled bookcase in cozy sitting area/ kitchen library puts cook books as well as novels close at hand for fireside reading.*
Architect: J. Allen Sayles.

*Dedicated to research and study, this library/office, off master bedroom, offers polished wood, plenty of light, and lots of space for books and periodicals.*
Architect: David S. Gast.

# Media,
# Fitness &
# Entertainment
# Areas

**W**hile recreation rooms are certainly not new to American homes, especially those with basements, the equipment likely to be found in such rooms is.

The electronics revolution has made high-quality audio and video components available at reasonable cost, tempting many people to set up rooms especially for listening and/or viewing. The development of portable, relatively lightweight fitness equipment has encouraged its relocation from the health spa to the house. And easy-maintenance acrylic spas and compact heaters for saunas make it possible for more people to install these valuable stress-reducing systems in their homes.

The challenge lies in designing spaces for such specific uses. Though accommodating a wide-screen television in a room may require only a few changes, turning an unused corner into a spa or sauna complex may demand extensive remodeling.

***Designing a media room.*** Most family rooms, of course, have the potential to incorporate electronic media. But if the compact disc system or wide-screen television and VCR are the main attractions, it makes sense to set them apart in order to get the most out of the equipment.

Probably the most important consideration with regard to audio equipment is the choice and location of the speakers. Try to select and position sound components so the sound will fill the room without overpowering it—and the rest of the house.

Seating makes a big difference, too, especially with the kind of sensitive speakers that "image" the sound, putting the listener right in the middle of the concert hall. Arranging seating that's right both for audio speakers and for viewing a video screen may be a problem, however. For instance, it's best to position a screen where light shining in through windows won't wash out the picture. But that doesn't always work with optimum speaker placement. Ex-

*Rich blue ceiling and walls lend drama to this multipurpose media room. Track lighting illuminates bookshelves, fills room with reflected light without creating glare on television. Built-in window seats conceal storage space.*
Design: Connie Sterne Associates.

periment with your equipment until you come up with the best possible arrangement.

**Fitness rooms, spas, and saunas.** Location is all-important when you're planning spaces for exercising and bathing. A fitness room, ideally, should be near a shower, spa, or dressing area, but probably not too close to bedrooms or a den, where the noise could be disturbing. Large windows can offer both ventilation and a view.

Adding a media center, floor-to-ceiling mirrors, and perhaps a wet bar to the fitness room may motivate even more frequent workouts.

An indoor spa or sauna is much more difficult to locate than one outdoors. The best location is a private site near the master bedroom or fitness room and close to the outside, if plumbing connections are available nearby.

Even more crucial are weight and humidity concerns: standard flooring cannot support a filled tub's weight, and an efficient ventilation system is essential

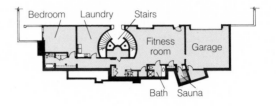

***Morning colors, soft light, and his and her exercise bicycles invite use of this attractive fitness room, enlivened with unexpected curves and angles.***
*Architect: Rob Wellington Quigley.*

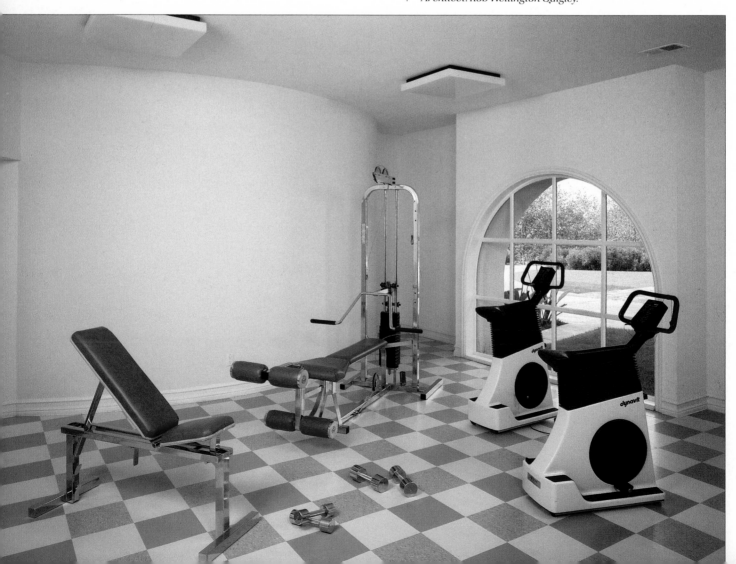

*Temperate outside, tropical inside: easy-maintenance indoor spa set into tile floor provides welcome humidity for plants in this glazed spa room.*
Architect: Peter C. Rodi, Designbank.

to control the heat and humidity generated by a spa. That's why probably the best time to think about an indoor spa is prior to new home construction or room addition.

***Rooms for children—and children at heart.*** Because games are popular at any age, making space for pool tables, chess games, or play-acting with stuffed animal friends is a high priority in many homes.

Such adult spaces might include comfortable seating areas, a wet bar, and even sliding doors that open to a patio or pool, a perfect formula for entertaining. Illumination can be soft, with direct lighting only over the game table.

For children, play space should be open and cheerful. Be sure to allow for lots of uninterrupted floor area for castle building, speedway racing, and board games. And when little heads begin to nod, have baskets, crates, and shelves close at hand for quick cleanups.

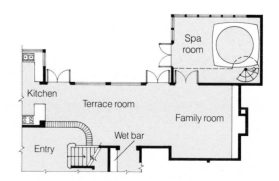

# Sleight of Hand

*Now you see it, now you don't—fully equipped media center occupies one end of spacious, sandy-hued garden room, hides behind doors when not in use.*

*Wide-screen television, potentially an imposing presence, reveals itself only when cabinet doors are opened. Other compartments store stereo components, VCR, records, and tapes in made-to-measure spaces.*

*With doors closed, audio and video equipment disappears behind stylish cabinetry designed to blend into room (below). Plush rug softens formal seating area. Wall of windows brightens space, makes dining practically alfresco (at right).*
Architect: Peter C. Rodi, Designbank.

# Silver Screen Magic

*Art Deco touches in high-tech screening room done in classic black and white recall glamor days of Hollywood when everything happened at the movies.*

*Making the most of a small space, family/media room offers plenty of seating and easy access to kitchen. When desired, natural light from windows in adjoining room flows in through blinds; track lighting does the rest. Room divider stores compact discs and tapes.*

*Red provides dramatic accent; overhead projector for television and VCR provides the drama. When last scene ends, screen rolls up, leaving space intact for other family pursuits. Closet neatly stacks stereo and video gear.*
Design: Minimal Space.

# Locating Audio & Video Gear

I n the past, audio and video equipment was plain looking and clunky, and often hidden behind cabinet doors. But the lean, arresting profiles and gleaming faces of today's components, with their LED readouts and colored lights that wink and flash, demand a wholly different treatment. Clearly, looking good is another of the equipment's wide array of functions.

When you're thinking about where to place your audio and video components, keep in mind that anything electronic has a distinct presence, for better or worse. How that presence fits your notion of ambience will affect both your choice of gear and the place that you design for it. Look carefully at the examples presented throughout this book for ideas you can adapt to your specific situation.

Whether or not the equipment is to be displayed, the layout of a media room needs to reflect certain requirements. The most obvious of these is the location of seating in relation to both the television and any audio speakers. The screen must be at a comfortable distance for viewing, and the speakers must be carefully positioned for best sound results. Less obvious, but equally important, is the need to place compact discs, tapes, records, and video cassettes near the appropriate recording or playback unit, for convenience (see drawing on facing page, at left).

*Video equipment.* Televisions and video monitors come in many shapes and sizes, but they all have to be plugged in and connected to antennae, cables and/or satellite receivers, VCRs, and sometimes stereo equipment. When planning video placement, give special attention to the location of electrical outlets and cables.

If a television or monitor is to be concealed in a cabinet or enclosure, make sure that it's well ventilated. Heat buildup eventually kills transistors and printed circuits. Because many sets have speakers on the side or rear of their cases, it's important to be sure the sound has an outlet (though an increasing number of new models are equipped with stereo receivers so their sound can go through the stereo system's speakers). One good way to get a television out of both an enclosure and traffic is to place it near the ceiling, either on a shelf or suspended from a bracket made especially for it (available where the set is sold).

Place a VCR unit near the television, where cable connections can be made easily and unobtrusively. A front-loading VCR can go under the set, but don't place a top-loader on top of the set; the television's heat is greater, and both units may be damaged.

Wide-screen televisions are generally silver screens on which a picture is projected, either from the front or rear. The equipment for the front-projection type needs to be placed directly in front of the screen, near the base, or on the ceiling. Sometimes, the unit can be put in a small hinged compartment under the floor. The gear for the rear-projection model is best concealed in a deep corner cabinet. If there's a closet or other unused space in the room next to the media room, a wide-screen television can be set into the wall with only the screen showing and operated exclusively by remote control.

*Stereo gear.* These days, a complete stereo system might include an amplifier, pre-amplifier, graphic equalizer, AM-FM tuner, compact disc player, cassette deck, and, conceivably, a turntable. All of that gear can be stacked, in or out of sight, in a stereo rack or in a piece of furniture, such as a desk or bookshelf, adapted to the task. Arrange the components and peripherals according to their serial connection; then drill holes as necessary to lead cables and wires out the back to a heavy-duty outlet strip equipped with a surge protector.

Use the ganglia model for organizing the wires and cables: play out just enough wire or cable to cover the required distance to a connection and

## Media Equipment Storage

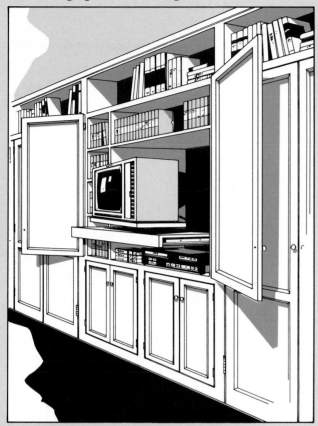

*Videotapes stack neatly around television and VCR. Television, mounted on pull-out shelf, swivels for easy viewing. Components hide behind cabinet doors when not in use.*

then wrap the rest in on itself with a twist-tie or rubber band, thereby avoiding the electronic spaghetti syndrome.

***Speakers and lighting.*** Speakers and lighting function in similar fashion, in that both sound and light need to be focused in the room. Many bookshelf-scale speakers have precise directional and frequency response properties that can make music sound three-dimensional in large areas of a room.

By using more than two speakers, strategically placed, you can focus a surround-sound effect on a particular seating area. If you coordinate the effect with a wide-screen television, the combined systems can place your private audience right in the concert hall or stadium.

Both music and television seem to be at their best in low to moderate light. The eye likes to wander while the ear tunes in, so it's nice to have framed

prints or other artwork on the walls, and sculpture, flower arrangements, or similar attractive objects on tables and surfaces. Light these with pencil-beam spots mounted on overhead tracks.

Watching television in complete darkness can lead to eyestrain; bright light and glare can have the same effect. Choose indirect illumination and focused beams that will enhance television viewing. To avoid glare, try to locate the screen so that windows aren't reflected on it.

Lighting is especially important in a room where a wide-screen television is located. Installing a dimmer switch allows you to bring down the house lights to the desired level when it's time for viewing.

## Shelf System for Compact Discs

*Adjustable track-and-bracket shelving holds an entire compact disc collection. Shelves are made from hardwood. Sliding dividers keep discs upright.*
*Design: Bill Richter.*

# Reflected Effects

*Mirrors help keep movements accurate and encourage efforts in these fitness rooms; large windows and white walls enlarge space.*

*Sighting on nearby oak keeps rowers on course in this second-story fitness room. Upholstered rest stool is a functional accent; wood floor reduces stress to joints and muscles. Oversize speakers can fill space with sound of crashing surf or a favorite aerobics rhythm.*
*Architect: Raymond M. Rooker. Interior design: Ruth Soforenko Associates.*

*Stylish exercise bar doubles as a towel rack. Behind mirrored sliding doors is storage space for weights and other equipment. Carpet muffles sound and cushions impact.*
Design: Minimal Space.

# Ideal Conditions

*Fully equipped fitness room with media center and outdoor spa engages the mind as well as the body.*

*Getting in shape is easier in a sleek, bright room. Large wall mirror, high ceiling with skylights, and recessed spots expand a narrow space.*

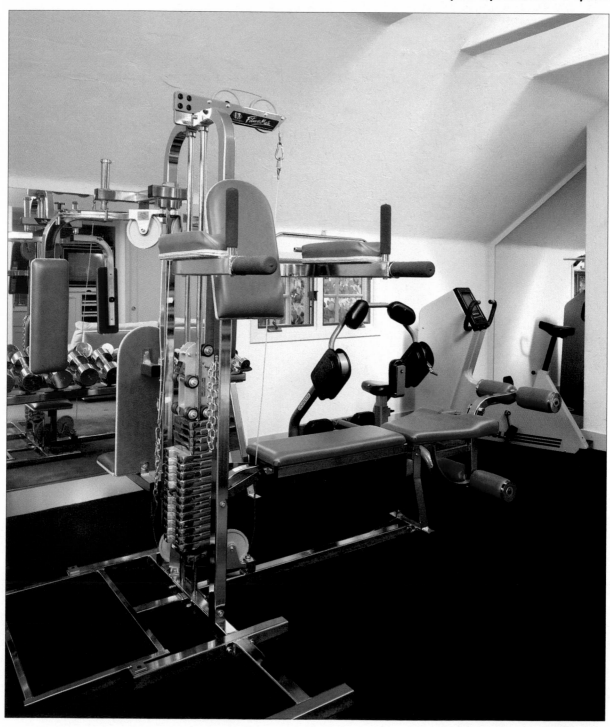

*Relief for sore muscles is just steps away from fitness room. Easy-maintenance spa (at right) is set flush with redwood deck. Cool-downs and rest periods between exercises are well spent in comfortable sitting area (below), outfitted with soft chairs, a wet bar, and a television on a pull-out shelf.*
Design: Heidi Hansen.

# Weights & Measures

Home fitness rooms achieve a perfect balance of practicality and style with sleek materials and bountiful light from a variety of sources.

*Expansive view motivates effort in this sunny corner fitness room. Wide mirror with brass stretching bar brightens space, provides personal perspective on workout.*
Design: Towers Interiors, Inc.

*Trophy case in corner of family room (at right) attests to success of fitness regimen. Locker colors echo carpet stripes. Mirror enlarges space, reflects light filtering through glass block windows (below).*
Architect: Moyer Associates Architects.

# At Your Leisure

*Stress management takes a backseat to sheer pleasure with in-house spa, sauna—or both.*

**Swim spa with a view combines a lap pool with a hot tub: high-powered jets at one end can be turned up, creating a current to swim against, or can bubble softly for a therapeutic massage. Curved glass enclosure adds to lighter-than-air effect.**
*Design: S. Robert Politzer.*

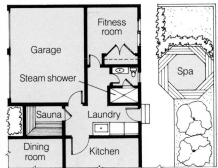

*Cedar sauna (at left) feels larger than it actually is. Benches accommodate people in varying positions, making the most of a small electric heater. Sauna adds finishing touch to a home fitness complex that includes adjacent steam shower, fitness room, and outdoor spa. Stereo system outside door (below), powers speakers under benches.*
Design: John Kolkka, Finnish-American Sauna.

# A Spa for All Seasons

*Sheltered indoor spas make the most of all kinds of weather, as well as keep maintenance costs down.*

**Set jewel-like into garden, sunspace with spa makes a virtue out of close quarters. Wide expanses of glass and repetition of color and line integrate spa with outside area.**
Design: Tim Magee, Rainshadow.

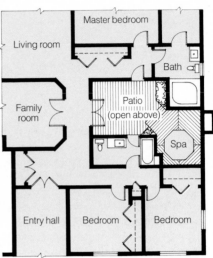

Situated in an awkward, unused space, elegant hot water retreat with a Japanese motif (at left) is centrally located, yet private. Shoji screens overhead mask openable skylights. Steps lead to an outside patio (below), so heat and humidity aren't problems.

Design: Keith Wallach.

# Adding a Wet Bar

A wet bar is more than just a nice touch. It can make a house seem more convivial, take pressure off the kitchen as an entertainment center, and keep hosts on the scene with their guests.

In simplest terms, a bar is a station from which liquid refreshments are served. The wet bar goes further, adding water and often electrical appliances to turn a simple bar into a small full-service area.

The components are standard: cabinets, a service counter, a working counter, and a sink with running water. A small refrigerator with an ice maker is useful, if you have room.

Beyond these essentials, you can add an almost unlimited variety of features. You may want to have a favorite beer on tap, along with soft drinks and mixers served via push-button siphon "gun." A large, powerful blender comes in handy. So do an instant hot water dispenser, an automatic high-output ice maker, a quick wine chiller, and an espresso machine.

It's convenient to have a range of wines on hand to suit varying tastes and occasions. Storing bottles in a wine rack is good, but it's better to use an insulated, temperature-controlled wine storage unit. A cruvinet, the vinous equivalent of a beer tap, keeps several open bottles of wine fresh for weeks while allowing you to draw off individual glasses as they're requested.

**Planning considerations.** A wet bar can be an island or peninsula in a room or can fit along a wall, but locating it may involve more than just picking a spot; there are functional considerations as well, such as water supply, drainage, and wiring.

Routing water supply pipes can be relatively easy if there's a crawlspace underneath the house, but it's difficult and expensive if the house is on a concrete slab. The same is true for tying a 1½-inch drainpipe into the home's existing drain-waste system. And if the sink is located far from an existing vent stack, you'll need to add a new vent that runs all the way up to the roof.

Another issue to consider is whether or not your existing electrical circuit is up to the added load of the wet bar's planned appliances and lighting. You may need a separate circuit for the refrigerator and new boxes for lighting. For help with plumbing and electrical concerns, call in a professional.

## Double-sided Shelf Unit

*Bottom of this shelving unit works, too. Make the most of space over a wet bar pass-through by affixing a slotted rack for glasses to underside of hanging shelves.*
Architect: John O'Brien of O'Brien & Associates.

**Design elements.** Once location has been determined, you can think about the storage needs of the wet bar and design cabinets accordingly. Devote separate cabinet areas to soft drinks and juices, aperitifs and cordials, cocktail liquors, mixers and garnishes, wines, and glassware. Stemware is best stored overhead, hung upside down in slotted racks (see illustration on facing page).

The service counter should be about 48 inches high and the working counter about 36 inches. Countertop materials can vary from natural and stained woods to polished stone, such as marble or granite.

You might choose a countertop sink that fits into a hole cut in a counter or an integral sink and countertop, a one-piece molded unit. Two sinks, of course, are better than one. The best faucet for a wet bar is a high gooseneck type with a rubber tip to protect glassware. Faucet handles come in many shapes and sizes; simple vertical levers are popular for wet bars.

An instant hot water dispenser, such as the one shown below, is helpful for preparing hot drinks and washing glassware. The half-gallon tank, which hangs on a bracket under the counter, taps the cold water supply through a valve and heats the water with an electric coil. The dispenser provides a steady flow of water at approximately 200°F (about 50° hotter than the average water heater's output). The power source is a grounded 120-volt outlet. When planning for such a unit, keep in mind that because the tank and output line will generate heat, they should be well clear of wine, liquor, and any liquids stored under pressure.

Illumination? Track lighting does the best job because you can focus beams straight down on the working counter. Light cabinet interiors with small fluorescent tubes on the undersides of shelves.

While you're wiring, consider installing an auxiliary tape deck or compact disc player behind the bar—but well away from splashing liquids. And don't forget to plan storage for the tapes or discs.

## Hooking Up a Wet Bar

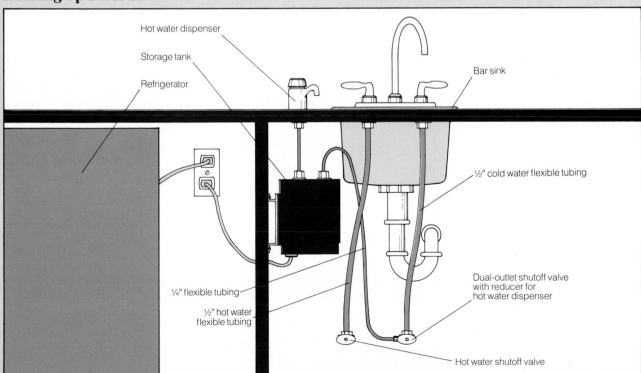

Hot water dispenser

Storage tank

Refrigerator

Bar sink

½" cold water flexible tubing

Dual-outlet shutoff valve with reducer for hot water dispenser

¼" flexible tubing

½" hot water flexible tubing

Hot water shutoff valve

*Electrical and plumbing connections beneath a wet bar require sound planning beforehand, especially if circuits or pipes must be extended. Instant hot water dispenser and mini-refrigerator, two useful additions to a wet bar, plug into a grounded receptacle. Flexible tubing connects faucets to water shutoff valves.*

# Multiple Diversions

*Plenty of light, a mélange of shapes, and complementary colors characterize this lively entertainment room, suitable for casual or formal use.*

*Unexpected angles create excitement in this airy entertainment room. Tile floor and rattan furnishings suggest the Tropics; pastel-colored fabrics and area rug add a contemporary touch.*

*Bar and garden room (above) open directly onto pool and garden. Pleasant sounds—soft clicks and whispers of balls on felt—of another kind of pool (at right) are amplified in bright, plush-carpeted alcove.*

Architect: Barry Fernald.

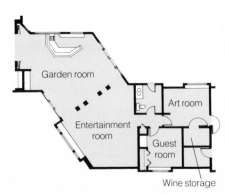

# A Room for All Reasons

*Airy and inviting, this gracious room serves many purposes, from quiet conversations to listening to music to large-scale entertaining.*

*Taking their cue from the out-of-doors, soaring conversation area (at right) and adjoining dining alcove (below) are done up in garden colors and patterns. Restful hues, light flooring and walls, and informal multipaned windows welcome family and friends alike.*

**Seating area faces blond natural-wood wet bar and cabinets for books, stemware, and media equipment (above). Television and stereo disappear behind cabinet doors when not in use (at left).**
*Architect: Alan Dreyfuss. Design: Nancy Holton, Surrey Interiors.*

# Equipment Storage

A place for everything, and everything in its place. A nice sentiment, but as any sailor will tell you, much easier said than done. Aboard ship, every spare cubic centimeter of hull space may be devoted to stowage, but stowing equipment at home is often haphazard and inefficient. But it doesn't need to be. Clutter management is the key to livable rooms, and finding or creating storage space is the key to clutter management.

It doesn't take long to realize that a little ingenuity, in addition to commodious space, is required to deal with bulky or awkward objects. A baseball glove may fit into a bureau drawer, imparting a pleasant leathery fragrance to socks and tee-shirts. But what about a catcher's mask, a stack of weights, a slant board, or an exercise mat?

Think not only of the mess, but also of how it comes into being. When the kids take a break from one-on-one in the driveway or return from the neighborhood diamond or soccer field, they probably head to the family room to relive the game's high points. When board games have been won or lost or when the aerobics tape ends, the cards, dice, and hand weights probably land on the floor of the playroom or fitness room. These, then, are some of the possible locations where you may want to plan for additional closets, cabinets, drawers, or other types of storage spaces.

**Storage solutions.** Once you've surveyed your family's habits, you'll no doubt know exactly where storage is needed, as well as the shape it should take.

Box modules, shown at right, offer simple storage solutions in a recreation or fitness room. Easily constructed from ¾-inch plywood or particleboard, they stack neatly because they have complementary dimensions. Each rectangular box is exactly twice the length and the same height as the square boxes. You can make as many as you like, in the shape and size that are best for your needs.

The pieces are glued and nailed together, sanded, and finished with polyurethane or enamel. If you like, you can screw the stacked boxes to each other or to the wall.

Consider adding hinged or sliding doors, or even slide-out drawers, to one or more of the boxes to keep clutter out of view. A simple seat can be made by placing two or more boxes together and adding an upholstered plywood top.

Don't overlook the storage possibilities of a roomy window seat. The seat pictured on the facing page, at left, is more than just a cozy place to while away the hours. It was created when a deep shelving

## Stacking Box Modules

*Modular boxes stack in any configuration, providing easy storage and retrievability for records, games, toys, and sports equipment. Paint them to accent or blend with room's decor.*

## Window Treatment

*Wall system surrounding a wide window creates an instant window seat with storage space beneath. Seat can also be built with a hinged lid that lifts to reveal a concealed storage compartment.*

the wide shelves, while cubbyholes in the middle organize jump ropes, gloves, and other small items. Jackets hang neatly below on their own hooks. An alternative is to fit the cabinet with shelves that adjust on tracks and brackets.

## Customized Storage Cabinet

*Spaces of varying shapes and sizes accommodate objects that were designed for a specific use, not for ease of storage.*

Architect: Jeff Burleson of Cabell Childress Associates.

system was built all around a wide window. Books and decorative objects adorn the shelves. Sliding doors make the storage space under the seat easily accessible. Or you could build rows of wide drawers into the front of the box. Another option is to make the seat a hinged lid that opens up a clutter-hungry compartment convenient for storing large, bulky items.

Another easy storage solution is a floor-to-ceiling cabinet (see at right). The doors pivot on recessed hinges to reveal a wealth of stowing spaces of different shapes and sizes. The tall locker holds large or irregularly shaped objects, such as ski equipment or exercise boards; balls and bulky items fit well on

# Where the Elite Meet

Some entertainment rooms are like private clubs—membership is limited to family members and their privileged guests.

*The entire family can amuse itself in this well-equipped game room, complete with television and stereo setup. Track lighting highlights different activity areas.*
Architect: Moyer Associates Architects.

*It could be a yacht club or a hunting lodge, but it's actually a comfortable room with plenty of space for bumper pool. Wide-screen television in corner provides additional entertainment.*
Architect: Peter C. Rodi, Designbank.

# Double Play

*Furniture and surfaces that serve more than one purpose are keys to playrooms that are fun and look good, too.*

*Built-in shelves in closet organize toys, adding color and lively interest to room decor. Simple two-tone area rugs unifies color scheme, protect floor in heaviest traffic areas.*
Design: Brenda Anderson and Kay Connelly of Keeping Traditions, Inc.

*Split-level playroom offers stepped surfaces that rise gradually to window seat and view. Soft cotton futon in alcove is perfect for tumbling, naps, or quiet play. Fireplace is closed off with child-safe doors.*
*Architect: William B. Remick.*

# Index